FROM SCRATCH

CREATE YOUR RECIPE FOR HAPPINESS AND
SUCCESS IN BUSINESS

ELIZABETH POOLEY

Copyright © 2022 Elizabeth Pooley

Cover Design by Kelly Laine Designs

ISBN: 979-8-9871329-0-6 (paperback edition)
ISBN: 979-8-9871329-1-3 (hardcover edition)

All rights reserved. This book or any portion thereof may not be reproduced or used in any manner without the express written permission of the author/publisher except for the use of brief questions in a book review.

Published by JEM Publishing

This book is dedicated to my children, Madison and Jack Pooley. They have inspired me to move past my adversities, to continue working hard, and never give up. My daughter's wisdom at such a young age has proven to be a re-awakening for me. My son's spirit is so like mine and has helped reveal a better understanding of myself. And to Blake, who came into my life much later as a bonus son. I could not have asked for three better children whom I respect so much. Thank you for your constant love and support.

CONTENTS

Introduction	vii
1. One Pound Motivation	1
2. Two Cups Opportunity	19
3. Three Pints Determination	27
4. Four Quarts Leadership	41
5. Five Dashes Grace	49
6. Six Tablespoons Self-care	55
7. Seven Teaspoons Optimism	65
8. Eight Ounces Wisdom	75
Conclusion	85
Acknowledgments	91
About the Author	93

INTRODUCTION

Dreams are an important facet of life. They can serve as an escape, especially from negativity, or they can serve as a source of excitement and motivation. Everything you do is because of a dream you have or once had in the past. The difference between a dream and hope is that fulfilling a dream requires you to act, while hope is a more passive aspiration. People who actively chase their dreams share specific behaviors: they take advantage of opportunities, they don't skip steps, they embrace challenges, they help others along the way, and they stay focused on their dream.

This is a story about my courage, perseverance, and faith. My dream has always been to create safe, welcoming, beautiful spaces that bring joy. It may sound simple, but this dream is the result of a complex childhood that lacked

Introduction

security and control, which ultimately, I believe, formed my entrepreneurial spirit. I have founded three successful businesses, with a fourth underway, all based on that dream—a dream I didn't always realize I was chasing. Now that I have stepped back and reflected on my personal and professional journey, I'm able to identify what it took to achieve my dream. Life is the greatest school I've attended. Through experience comes wisdom, and wisdom makes you a great teacher. I want to share the wisdom I've learned as an entrepreneur so you don't feel alone in your journey toward achieving your dream, whether personal, professional, or spiritual.

I also hope to be an inspiration and help you discover what makes you happy so you can actively pursue that dream. I have two mottos in life: Don't ever give up. Don't skip steps. You might have to pivot, pause, or walk away, but don't give up trying. Your dream might not always look like what you originally envisioned, but often it ends up being better in the end. If you skip steps in an attempt to reach your dream faster, you'll miss opportunities that provide the vital experience and understanding necessary to truly fulfill your dream. Skipping steps also results in duplicating efforts. I hate doing things twice. It's a waste of time, and time is valuable. I want to do something once and give it all I have. Doing something right the first time is a reflection of your principles. Many people have joined me from one business venture to the next because they know that whatever I put my heart and soul into, it will be a valuable experience.

There are more than 32 million small businesses in the U.S. That's a lot of dreams! Unfortunately, nearly half of all small businesses fail within the first five years, according to an October 2018 article in *Forbes*, "What Percentage Of Small Businesses Fail—And How Can You Avoid Being One Of Them?" If you're an aspiring entrepreneur, a current business owner, or working for a small business, I want to help you navigate your role by providing insight, ideas, and ways for you to become the best version of yourself. In doing so, I hope you validate what you've already experienced, realize that your leadership style needs to change, or gain a better understanding of what a small business owner faces on a daily basis. No matter the dream you're trying to achieve, there are certain characteristics you must have to reach your goals. When you combine these characteristics, or "ingredients," you'll be able to create your own recipe for happiness and success.

The first ingredient in your recipe is *motivation*—the underlying passion that constantly drives you toward happiness and success. One of the best ways to identify your true motivation is by looking at your past, which is an effective predictor of the future. Activities, hobbies, and early motivators you had as a child can be used as a roadmap toward identifying and reaching your dream.

The next ingredient in your recipe is *opportunity*. Don't

Introduction

say no to an opportunity just because it doesn't fit within your current vision. Every opportunity is like a stepping stone toward a new skill or a different perspective. Don't be afraid of a negative experience—some of the best opportunities arise during adverse situations.

Determination is another important ingredient. Most entrepreneurs are competitive and excellent problem-solvers. Challenges motivate an entrepreneur to solve problems effectively and efficiently as they occur. The key is to not let perfectionism get in the way. When you embrace adversity and keep moving forward to the best of your ability, you'll find that you can solve problems faster.

I live by the belief that you should treat others the way you want to be treated. The most successful business owners and employees approach customers and each other with patience, empathy, and effective communication skills. A strong leader must be able to demonstrate those qualities at the appropriate moments while also maintaining their authority. I believe these qualities are lacking in today's world, which is why strong *leadership* is a critical ingredient.

You are often your own worst critic. Sometimes it's necessary to stop and give yourself the next ingredient —*grace*. Everyone makes mistakes, and decisions don't always pan out. It's okay to take a step back, regroup, go back to basics, and start going through the steps one at a time until you're back on track. When you and your employees realize mistakes are part of the process, growth and success happen faster.

A common shared experience among many small business owners is wearing themselves down physically and mentally. If your health declines, your business can't sustain success. It takes a healthy person to lead, so *self-care* is an essential ingredient. Establishing boundaries and a work-life balance is critical to achieving your dream, and ignoring self-care can create a domino effect that cascades into your personal life.

Dreams are rarely achieved without a healthy dose of *optimism* on the ingredient list. For many entrepreneurs, optimism takes many forms. An optimist is always creating, inventing, and brainstorming their next idea. As long as you remain true to your motivation and clear about your definition of happiness and success, then simple optimism is enough at the moment. Optimism implies you have confidence in the future—a future you create for yourself.

Dreams are meant to be shared with those around you. My dreams involve creating things that make others happy. Once you've reached your dream, listen to those around you, whether co-workers, family, or friends, and help them identify what makes them happy—make *wisdom* part of your recipe. You can also become a mentor at work, at school, or within a local organization. Providing support, whether educational, emotional, or financial, is critical to a thriving

Introduction

community. Starting from scratch isn't easy, so I want to work together to create your recipe for happiness and success to help make your dreams come true.

1
ONE POUND MOTIVATION

Many small business owners say they stumbled into their business by accident. That's partially true. If you dive into their past, you are likely to discover a correlation between their past and present. There will be a common thread between activities, hobbies, and previous jobs/business ventures that defines the passion that motivates and drives them. They may be looking for a way to solve a problem they experienced in one of these areas. If you look at your own past, you can probably find one primary motivator that became the driving force for your dreams.

#Childhood

My childhood influenced every business I've owned. I

grew up in an unstable home environment where at a young age, I took on a caregiver role for the adults around me. My homelife was messy and traumatic, so to compensate, I took solace in creating a calming environment—one that resembled a happy Norman Rockwell painting. My mother often commented that I liked to make everything look "pretty." One Christmas during elementary school, we didn't have many presents under the Christmas tree. I found a bunch of tiny boxes and wrapped them with scraps of paper and ribbon and placed them throughout the tree as ornaments to make it appear as though there were little presents all over the tree. I then dreamt about selling those as ornaments. I loved wrapping gifts so they looked like expensive gifts from a department store. Receiving an exquisitely wrapped gift felt rich and regal regardless of what was inside.

As a latchkey kid, I often had to make my breakfast and lunch, especially during the summers when my mother was working. Sometimes I entertained myself by creating a formal table similar to those in Norman Rockwell paintings. I'd place the silverware, plate, and napkin on the table and occasionally put a flower in a vase. If I cooked a frozen dinner, I scooped it out of the foil container onto a plate so it looked fancier. We didn't have much money growing up, so nice things were a luxury. We lived in a two-bedroom, low-income townhouse. I felt wealthy when we moved to a three-bedroom unit in the same complex. Plus, I no longer had to share a bedroom with my brother.

In middle school, I realized our home wasn't as nice as other people's, so to make it look nicer, I painted the walls, hung wallpaper border around the rooms, and planted flowers outside. I wanted our home to look like a picture in a magazine. My parents loved me, but they were not always able to provide the safety, care, and abundance I so desperately craved. However, my grandmother provided a stable source of love and comfort. She was patient and kind and taught me how to cook, garden, and appreciate hard work. Her influence and my need to create welcoming spaces set the stage for my entire life, career, and my dreams. My grandmother was an integral part of my character development.

#Entrepreneur

In seventh grade I played intramural basketball and wanted a pair of brand name basketball shoes like the other players. We couldn't afford them, so I came up with a way to buy them myself. One day I stopped in the local pet shop and noticed the baby hamsters. I asked the owner where he got them, and he told me people bred them and sold him the babies. Suddenly I knew how I was going to make money for my shoes—I'd become a hamster breeder.

That year I asked for a male and female hamster for my

birthday and was shocked when I received them. I had no idea how to breed hamsters, so I just put them in a cage together. I woke up one morning a few weeks later and found a nest of babies in the cage. I was thrilled and went off to school. When I came home later that day, the babies were gone without a trace. I returned to the pet shop and the owner explained that female hamsters often eat their first litter of babies. He told me the next litter should survive. I was mortified!

I returned home and tried again. A short time later, another litter of babies was born. This time the babies survived and grew. When they were big enough, I put them in a McDonald's Happy Meal box and took them to the pet shop. I sold them for $1.50 each. I kept breeding my hamsters and selling the babies to the pet store until I had enough money to buy the basketball shoes. I expected the other girls to think I was cool when I wore the shoes to school for the first time. I soon realized they didn't care that I had new shoes—I was the only one who cared. Even though I had worked hard and earned those shoes, it didn't leave me with the feeling I had hoped for because the effort didn't benefit anyone other than myself—an important lesson about the relationship between success and happiness. I also learned another important lesson—success is born out of necessity because I wasn't born into opportunity.

. . .

#Confidence

By the time I reached high school, my homelife had deteriorated to a point where I fell in with the wrong crowd. I was headed down a dangerous path when my dad pulled me aside and told me he wanted to put me in modeling school, which was something I had always talked about when I was younger. I knew it was expensive, and the thought made me nervous, but my dad insisted. I also secretly saw it as a way out of the bad scene in which I was living, and I quickly embraced the idea.

I shopped thrift stores for designer clothes, learned how to apply makeup, and kept scrapbooks of fashion articles from *Vogue* and other magazines. The highlight of the experience was the photoshoot for my portfolio—I was in awe at seeing myself in such a different way. Those pictures didn't show my homelife or reflect our economic status. For the first time, I believed I could be anything I wanted.

One day my dad suggested I enter the Miss Teen Nebraska pageant. Modeling was one thing, but I wasn't interested in pageantry. However, my modeling instructor convinced me to enter. With my parents' encouragement, I learned how to interview, walk, and dress but didn't take the pageant too seriously.

The day of the pageant, my dad dropped me off at the local hotel where it was held. I met all the contestants, and we were briefed on the itinerary. Later that day, it was time for the interviews. I changed into my interview outfit—a beautiful champagne-colored sweater and shimmery skirt with matching dyed satin heels. During the shopping trip with my father, every time I looked at a price tag, I glanced at him. He never wavered. He only said, "If you like it, we will buy it." I never knew how my parents scraped together the money to afford my pageant clothes, but I appreciated it.

During the pageant I was contestant number 9 and therefore wore that number all day. I entered the interview room and sat next to my instructor to wait my turn to interview with the judges. Out of nowhere, I was overcome with nerves and emotion and started to cry. My instructor calmly handed me a tissue, told me to take a breath, and promised everything would be fine. "And if not, you've gained an experience," she said. The first judge called me over, and I quickly dried my eyes and took a deep breath.

The first question the judge asked was, "How do you feel about being in front of nine judges?" I looked down at the number pinned to my sweater, shrugged, and said, "My number is nine, so I guess it's good luck." The judge chuckled, and I immediately relaxed. Eight more judges to go. I wasn't nervous the rest of the interview and answered the questions with ease. Afterward, the contestants had lunch together in the hotel ballroom. During lunch, I reached for a carafe of coffee, and when I poured, the lid fell off and coffee spilled all over my beautiful champagne-colored outfit. Despite my embarrassment, I pretended to shrug it off.

I spent the rest of the day wishing the other contestants good luck and encouraging them. I thought they were all more likely to win than I was. That night we stood on stage for the ceremony. I clapped as they called the names for the runners-up. When they finally announced the name of the winner, I kept clapping—I didn't realize it was me! When they placed the crown on my head as Miss Teen Nebraska, I was too shocked to cry. My family and modeling instructor were both proud of me. I went on to compete in the Miss Teen USA pageant but had no goals of winning. The realist in me felt pageants at that level were all rigged, but I went for the opportunity and had fun.

At nationals I was exposed to so many types of people. I spent most of my time watching and listening to how others navigated people and their environment. This was a whole new world for me. I met directors, producers, choreographers, and celebrities, including Frankie Valli, the Commodores, and the lead singer of The Turtles. It was cool to talk with celebrities. I learned so much about a world I had never been part of, but I caught on quickly how to interact within it. I learned how to be an extrovert, which is not my natural personality, but that skill would become critical in my future business endeavors.

#NATURE

My first job was working at a skeet range at age 14. A year

later, I landed a waitress job by telling the manger he could call my one reference (my mother), who would testify that I kept an exceptionally clean room. After high school, I worked for the National Pageant Association in Kansas City as a pageant mentor and coach for regional queens before moving on to the restaurant industry, both of which honed my communication and customer service skills.

Then at age 20 I found a job as a plant technician for an interior maintenance and landscape company—I watered and cared for plants at local business offices. That experience eventually inspired me to start my own interior landscape company at the age of 21 called E's Foliage and Flowers. I started with one watering bucket, a soil tester, pruners, and an apron. A friend designed my logo and business cards, and I bought a hatchback vehicle to accommodate my supplies. My sales tactic was to simply ask businesses to give me a chance—if they didn't like my service, they could fire me.

That business blossomed, and I had it for seven years. It perfectly fed my need to create welcoming, beautiful spaces. It also fit my personality. The introvert in me enjoyed the solace of caring for plants, but I was able to easily and comfortably communicate with my customers when needed thanks to my previous work experiences. Toward the end of ownership, I was also handling corporate Christmas decorating and plant installations for national restaurant chains. Plants filled my entire living room, and my husband at the time helped me as much as he could with the business.

However, pregnant with my second child, I realized it was time to move on. I advertised the business for $25,000, and ultimately sold it for $8,000—a significant profit considering I had zero overhead—and I promised my husband I wouldn't start another business until our second child was in kindergarten.

#Pumpkin Patch

I kept my promise to my husband for four years. During that time, I fully embraced my role as a mother and farm wife. For the first time, I was living in that Norman Rockwell painting—we were a happy family of four. I cooked three meals a day, helped with farm chores, and spent my free time soaking up nature and the outdoors. I finally found the security and comfort I had been trying to create my entire life.

My husband's family owned and operated three farms, one of which was ours. As my in-laws grew older and needed care, I was quick to help them. Unfortunately, as their health declined, they needed skilled nursing care, which required them to sell their primary farm. Because the family's operations centered around that farm, including ours, I knew our lives were going to change. Suddenly, the financial and emotional security we had created was in jeopardy. As I watched the developer tear down my in-laws' old barn, fear and anxiety crept in.

With few farming capabilities on our own other than bailing hay and a small cattle operation, resources dried up. At Christmas we had little money for gifts, so I baked homemade cookies to give to my kids' teachers, friends, and other groups in lieu of gifts (I continue my Christmas cookie baking tradition to this day). On a few occasions, we had to get groceries at the local food pantry. My need to preserve financial and emotional security grew tenfold. We needed income, and I wanted to remain a stay-at-home mom. As usual throughout my life, when my security was threatened, rather than retreat I faced the challenges head on. I asked myself, "How can we monetize this farm and ensure we can keep living here?"

Fall has always been my favorite season, especially on the farm. There's nothing more perfect than a hot cup of coffee on a crisp fall morning, walking the property surrounded by chickens, livestock, and fresh dew on the fields. One of my favorite fall activities had always been visiting Vala's Pumpkin Patch—a farm stand turned family entertainment destination located about 30 minutes away from my home. Why not create my own pumpkin patch on a smaller scale? I grabbed a notebook and recorded everything I needed to start that business: finances, equipment, and employees. I walked around our farm and envisioned where each activity would be placed. Though we had no money, as soon as I had the vision, I knew it would be a success. My only obstacle was to get the right people to believe in me and invest.

The most resistance came from my husband. He'd never been to Vala's and couldn't understand why anyone would pay money to visit our farm. I walked him around the property, explaining my vision, and he just couldn't see it. Finally, I laid it all on the line and told him the only way we could keep the farm was to make money by starting a business. Our two options were a pumpkin patch or I was going to open a restaurant (after all, I had years of restaurant experience). He pointed out that if I started a restaurant, I'd never be home, so he agreed to the pumpkin patch. "Let me make a success of our farm and carry on the Pooley name," I said. Pooley's Pumpkin Patch was born.

After getting my husband's buy-in, I needed money to start the business. I presented my plan to my brother-in-law, father-in-law, and two others in the community, and collectively they invested $20,000. We already had tractors, space to grow pumpkins, and a large barn. I bought pumpkin seeds, scales to weigh the pumpkins, cash registers, and a couple of ponies for pony rides. A friend of mine had previous experience at pumpkin patches and offered to help me get started. In the fall of 2004 (a year before my son started kindergarten), we opened to the public with very little to offer other than pony rides, a giant tire swing, chickens, and pumpkins. But unlike Vala's with its massive crowds, we were perfectly suited for families with small children.

We started marketing to that demographic and highlighting the fact we were a small, working farm. My daughter groomed the ponies, my son tended to the chickens in the coop, and my husband worked in the field. As word spread and the number of customers grew, we did too, adding toy tractors for small children to ride, face painting, and local vendors selling goods in the barn. The energy was positive and wholesome. We rapidly grew and continued to expand. That's when my marriage started to fall apart.

When you own a business with your spouse, it's important to be on the same page. We had different ideas for our future. Thus began the fray. We tried counseling, but it didn't help. We grew apart each day. Our marriage deteriorated to the point where divorce seemed to be the only option for me. But I knew if we divorced, I would lose the pumpkin patch. We were finally reaching incredible sales and making a profit. I had built our farm into a successful business that could sustain us for the rest of our lives. So, I held on for a few more years, constantly struggling with the decision, hoping things would change and that we could work it out.

In 2010, seven years after opening, I filed for divorce. I desperately wanted to keep the pumpkin patch going and offered to either buy or lease the land from my husband. He said no. The only concession he made was that he would move out of the house so the kids and I could continue to live there until they both had graduated from high school. Sadly, Pooley's Pumpkin Patch closed. Losing that business felt like another failure on top of my divorce. I withdrew from the community because I was embarrassed the business had closed and felt like people thought less of me. My kids had grown up at the pumpkin patch, and between its closing and the divorce, their lives were negatively impacted. For years I tried to find a way to resurrect it, but it wasn't meant to be.

Suddenly, I was a single mom who needed income. I took an office job at the church preschool. I worked hard at it but have never been suited for a desk job—it's too restrictive and doesn't provide the freedom to be creative and interact with people the way I wanted. Over time, my spirit faded and I felt numb. Every day after work, I went home, fed the kids, and went to bed. Some nights I didn't even make dinner. I felt like I had no purpose in life. The farm was a skeleton of its former self—the cattle had been sold, the chickens were gone, and the barn was falling apart. I put on weight and stopped taking care of myself. My kids felt the anxiety and witnessed the changes. Again, I found myself at the end of my rope, desperate for security.

#**GRIND**

My kids were the only bright spot in my life, and one of my favorite activities was getting coffee with my daughter.

She taught me the difference between a cappuccino and macchiato, and I was fascinated by the variety of coffee drinks. Plus, coffee shops were naturally warm. They offered the sense of safety and security that I was desperate to find. When faced with a sink or swim situation, what did I do? I swam toward a new business idea. This time, I decided to open a coffee shop despite being broke and knowing nothing about the coffee industry. I spent months envisioning the shop and knew the dilapidated car wash next to the local gas station in my town was the perfect location. I also had the perfect name: Grinders Coffee.

Desperate times call for desperate measures, and the only viable investor I could think of was my father. We didn't have a close relationship, and deep down I felt it was a bad idea, as our visions had rarely aligned, but it was my only option. Being an optimist, I thought it would bring us closer together. He agreed to invest when I asked, but quickly wanted to be a full partner in the business. I didn't have the courage to argue against a partnership out of fear he would pull his funding if I didn't agree to his role as a partner rather than an investor. I was out of options and desperate to create financial security. From this experience, I learned never to allow desperation to sway your decisions. Because I refused to put my name on the loan, he made it impossible for me to spend the money the way I needed to build a successful business. We purchased the car wash, leveled it, and I started working with an architect to design the coffee shop.

Unfortunately, my dad didn't agree with most of my choices and created obstacles every step of the way.

He argued with the architect. He hired his own less-expensive contractor with little commercial experience. He burned bridges with members of the city council, the Omaha Housing Authority, and the owners of the gas station adjacent to our future business. He argued with customers at the gas station about parking—the same customers I was hoping to capture through partnerships with the gas station owners. Bit by bit he ruined relationships in the community as well as the reputation that went with my name. The final straw occurred one day while driving and I couldn't immediately answer his texts. He was so angry he couldn't contact me, that when I finally returned the call, he gave me an ultimatum that it was his way or no way.

I sat on my porch swing and cried, grieving the loss of another business. My father had already put my name and reputation in jeopardy, so I knew I couldn't keep working with him. Instead, I borrowed a friend's truck, drove to the nearly finished coffee shop, and removed everything I owned—tables, chairs, the business plan, and my detailed notes. I left the keys on the counter, texted him, and wished him good luck. I went home, stowed the furniture in the barn and then posted on social media that I was no longer associated with Grinders Coffee. I was devastated. The shop opened but was up for sale within months. Once again, hoping to resurrect what I knew could be a successful business, I asked my dad if I could buy or lease the space. He refused and sold the building to somebody else. It was another heartbreak. I was back to feeling like a failure, broke, and worried that my kids and I couldn't continue to live on the farm we so loved. My sense of security was threatened yet again, but this time, I decided that if I opened another business and it failed, it was going to be solely because of me and nobody else. No more depending on other people.

Ingredient Tip: Blend the Past with the Present

Each time my businesses closed unexpectedly, it felt like a failure and easy for others to point out my lack of success. Looking back, I realize that every concept was viable and successful in its own right. Each experience in life serves as a stepping stone full of valuable lessons that eventually blend to provide the motivation you need to succeed and ultimately find happiness. One of the biggest takeaways from my previous businesses is the realization that I have all the experience necessary to run a successful business. I have proven that I can create amazing concepts. I have the work ethic and the drive to succeed and win. As long as I'm in the driver's seat, I know that I can make my businesses sustainable. Ambitious people don't look back at what they've done; they look forward to what they haven't done yet.

It's also clear that I start businesses as a way to create a sense of security and stability for myself and my family, which translate into a safe, welcoming, stable space for others and their families. Starting a business may seem like one of the riskiest things you can do, but for me, it's less risky than never trying. Financial security doesn't mean money will make you happy or that it solves your problems; it means you are able to provide for yourself and others. That feeling is what results in happiness—something everyone needs regardless of upbringing. Understanding how your past contributes to your present motivation is an important ingredient in the recipe for happiness and success in business.

2

TWO CUPS OPPORTUNITY

So often in life, the best opportunities present themselves when you're not looking. Like many entrepreneurs, I jump on board without a lot of analysis, because overthinking can stall growth. One of the best pieces of advice I can give is to never pass up an opportunity. Each opportunity provides a skill set, and even if you don't feel it serves a purpose at the time, it will probably be one you need down the road. An opportunity could also turn out to be the very thing you need to fulfill your dreams.

#Searching

Shortly after my exit from Grinders, my agreement with my ex-husband to remain on the farm was coming to an end. In May 2018, my daughter Maddie graduated from college, and my son Jack graduated from high school. He was planning to attend NYU in Shanghai, China, which meant I had to move off the farm by August. My sense of security cracked and anxiety bubbled, which sparked my need to start another business to ensure survival.

I flew to Auburn, Alabama, to help Maddie move back home after her graduation. Our final morning there, a friend of hers made us breakfast and bought a box of donuts from D2, a local donut shop. I opened the box and was surprised to see the donuts were square instead of round. I don't care for sweets in the morning, but I was intrigued and took a bite. The donut was incredibly soft, not overly sweet, and so good! I ate the entire donut, and then another, and another. I oohed and aahed over those donuts. Maddie's friend explained D2 was a tiny mom and pop donut shop. I left very impressed but didn't give it another thought.

I returned home and spent the next few months preparing to leave the farm and move into a residential house in a suburban neighborhood. I also accompanied Jack to the University of New York's campus in Shanghai, China, where he was starting school in the fall. Leaving your child halfway across the world is gut-wrenching, and coming home and saying good-bye to the farm was the emotional icing on the cake. I walked around the property and kissed the tire swing one last time. Moving into the new house immediately felt claustrophobic, which further fueled my desire to start a new business in hopes of returning to country living.

A few months later, Maddie's friend in Auburn texted me and said that D2 Donuts was for sale. I responded, *Lol. Thanks, but I don't want to buy a donut shop, and I'm not moving to Auburn.* He texted back with the owner's name and number, *just in case,* and I thanked him. Owning a donut shop in another city seemed like the most absurd idea and a horrible fit for me. I didn't even like sweets!

The financial insecurity of owning a new house and not working full time set in, and about two months later, with no expectation, I called the owner of D2 Donuts. I told him I had tried his donuts and loved them, but I really wasn't interested in owning a donut shop or moving to Alabama. He encouraged me to visit his shop for a chat. With no other business prospects on the horizon, I agreed. It couldn't hurt, right? I traveled to Auburn and met the owner, who introduced me to his operation. The donuts were awesome, but the shop wasn't making enough money to meet my needs. I knew I could make it successful and immediately obsessed over how to do that.

I visited Auburn several more times, and each time I told myself I didn't want to own a donut shop and I definitely wasn't moving to Auburn with its high heat and humidity. Every night I prayed about what to do, and every night the answer was the same: I needed to do it. That's when I decided the only way to make it feasible was to bring the donut shop to Omaha. I mentioned the idea to the owner, and he said, "If you think you can do something with this in Omaha, then do it." I had no idea what I was doing or if I could make it work. Through extensive notes, videos, and pictures, I learned his entire process in three visits. I could envision the new name, the new logo, and decided to buy the business. I negotiated the asking price because I wanted only the equipment and the recipes. He agreed. Within 30 days he closed the shop in Auburn and shipped everything to me—including the paperclips from his desk. I stuffed it into a storage unit and now owned another business. It was an opportunity I couldn't pass up.

#Excitement

A business isn't successful because of an idea; it's successful due to the execution of that idea. I knew I had to execute on all points to make my new business viable. At my age, I felt this was my last shot. The first task was to find a space in Omaha for the shop. I envisioned the "pretty" aspects—the colors, the feel, and even the style of furniture. I found the perfect storefront and quickly hired an architect, a contractor, and applied for permits. The process became a whirlwind of decisions from locations for electrical outlets to the placement of doors. Though it happened at break-neck speed, every decision was mine. This time, nobody was getting in my way.

Two Cups Opportunity

In December 2018, Jack came home from college in China for Christmas. Adapting to school there had presented many challenges, and he decided not to return. Instead, he wanted to help me open the business, and I was ecstatic to have him back in the U.S. He also proved to be a huge help. Together, we spent months disassembling each piece of equipment and cleaning every part by hand. It was painstaking but necessary work. I continued to set up all aspects of the business, meeting with the city and my contractor regularly. I had an active role in every detail of my shop and business, both literally and figuratively building the foundation.

#NoFear

The community began to buzz about what was going to open in the space, and I insisted the exterior sign not go up until 30 days before we opened. In June 2019, I started paying rent on the shop, confident we'd be open by fall. That didn't happen. No matter how much careful planning you do, there are always unexpected obstacles. Because space in the shop was limited, I wanted a unisex bathroom that both employees and customers could use. City codes dictated that I needed two separate bathrooms, which forced me to redesign the kitchen. I also discovered that I needed two hand sinks instead of one, which meant less working space near the cashier station. I installed an additional HVAC system—one for the kitchen and one for the dining room—because the two spaces had to be kept at different temperatures. Each obstacle snowballed into another, causing additional delays and added expense. By the time I was ready to decorate the shop's dining room, I was out of money and ended up doing it myself for about $200.

The exterior sign went up in January 2020, and 30 days later we still weren't open. I needed to hire and train staff, but it had been nearly a year since I had been trained. I wasn't sure I knew how to train the staff or if I could get the shop up and running. But I had committed to this opportunity and refused to get caught up in overthinking. I needed to keep going. The previous owner traveled to Omaha and helped place the equipment in the shop, then re-trained us how to mix the dough, roll it, cut the donuts, fry them, and glaze them. As an entrepreneur, you need to remind yourself that you bought a business, not a job; hiring staff is key in order for you to operate your business.

#SquareDonut

In March 2020, with a skeleton staff and a vague idea of what we were doing, we sent out invites for a soft opening. We invited friends, family, and colleagues—about 100 people total, hoping 50 would attend. We held it on two consecutive days, one during the day and one during the evening to capture the after-work crowd. Because the staff needed to practice taking orders, boxing product, and working the cash register, we priced everything for $1. I printed comment cards and asked for feedback on every aspect, from the quality of the donuts to the flow of traffic to the shop's ambiance.

The soft opening was a huge success. We had about 100 people attend, including some "crashers" who hadn't received invites but wanted to be part of it. Social media coverage exploded, and the feedback was overwhelmingly positive. People loved the donuts, the atmosphere of the shop, and the customer service. A few people commented that some of the donuts were more rectangular than square, and some of the tables and chairs didn't match (part of my limited décor budget), but those were all things I wanted to hear and could fix. I was relieved when it was over because I felt like my vision had been seen and appreciated, especially at a time when there was so much donut competition in town. We all got our jitters out and had less anxiety about opening to the public. I knew it was just the first step of the journey and we had to keep focused and moving forward.

Ingredient Tip: Add More Opportunity as Desired

There are opportunities around every corner and each serves a purpose. Success only happens when you take advantage of opportunities, so don't hesitate to try one or more that come along. Once you do pursue an opportunity, see it through. The minute you stop, question, doubt, and let fear sink in is when you fail. The best defense is offense, and success means always moving forward even if you're unsure of what lies at the end. I didn't have the luxury of stopping to reflect —I was in survival mode. I needed Square Donut's doors to open so I could regain my financial and emotional security. There was no other option. The fear of not having security was much greater than the fear of opening a new business and having it fail. Grabbing opportunities and being fearless in seeing them through is a critical component in the recipe toward achieving your dreams.

3

THREE PINTS DETERMINATION

Author and motivational speaker Christine Caine said, "Sometimes when you are in a dark place, you think you've been buried, but actually you've been planted." I think this statement applies to many situations when facing challenges and adversity. The difference between feeling buried and planted is determination. I've had many times in my life when determination is the only thing that prevents me from giving up. Entrepreneurs are competitive by nature and good problem solvers. When faced with a challenge, they tackle it head-on and push through because they want to succeed and ultimately win. Determination—and plenty of it—is a critical ingredient for chasing your dreams.

. . .

#Pivot

Two days after Square Donut's soft opening, Covid-19 hit Omaha, and the state issued its Covid-19 mandates. Restaurants could remain open for takeout only—customers had to be in and out within 10 minutes. Up to that point, I was laser-focused on single donut sales, which meant customers being able to browse the donuts in the case and order at their leisure. How was I supposed to ensure that customers would be in and out of the shop within 10 minutes? The only solution I could think of was to offer pre-selected boxed donuts. It sounds easy, but how do you select donuts that everyone will like? Personally, I'd never buy a box of donuts I couldn't pick out myself.

I opted for five different boxes based on price. Not only did I have to train the staff on how to fill these pre-made boxes, but we had to train customers on each option. I even made a video for social media with instructions on how to order donuts. This was unprecedented for the industry. It was the only way I could keep my doors open during the beginning of the pandemic. Unfortunately, some customers weren't so understanding. They yelled at staff when told they were unable to choose their own donuts. They told me the shop would fail. They posted horrible, angry comments all over social media, trying to destroy my credibility even though they didn't know me personally. People reacted to the fear and uncertainty of the pandemic in hateful ways. Instead of feeling like a failure, I focused on the pivot because it was my only choice. I worked harder, determined to succeed even in this new Covid-19 climate. I responded to every hateful social media comment with grace and thoughtful explanation. I had extensive conversations and invited angry customers to return to the shop for another experience. Protecting my business, my employees, and my reputation drove me to become more transparent. The pandemic changed the landscape for small business owners and their employees: we were now seen as human beings affected by the pandemic just like everyone else.

With more and more restaurants closing, we did what was in our power to remain open, and customers' initial anger died down. Sales climbed and then began to soar. Maintaining customer service is always crucial, but now it was critical. We were open seven days a week, and most days a line formed out the door. Soon the line extended down the sidewalk. We fell into a groove, and customers raved about our pre-selected boxes. I worked as hard as I could and kept driving forward to succeed.

Then, three months later, the 10-minute mandate lifted, and we were allowed to fill the cases with donuts and provide single sales. On the one hand this was great news—we could finally operate as a normal donut shop. On the other hand, staff only knew how to fill pre-made boxes, so they needed to be re-trained. I made price tags for each product, decided where to put the donut trays, and revisited pricing for custom boxes. Customers also had to be re-trained. Some were unhappy that we no longer offered the pre-made boxes. We introduced the Dealer's Choice box, which meant employees could choose the donuts that went into the box. This made some employees nervous, so I devised a chart—each box required a maximum of three specialty donuts, at least two cake donuts, and the rest any type of square donut as long as two had sprinkles. The entire transition from pre-made boxes to single sales was rough, but it paid off.

Single sales began blowing up. They were bigger than sales from the pre-selected boxes. Lines were even longer now. People re-emerged after being on lockdown for three months and they wanted donuts. I staffed 18 people on the weekends to keep up with demand and couldn't wait for Tuesday and Wednesday when the shop was less busy and I could catch my breath. But on those busy days, the energy, vibe, and positivity were infectious. If someone dropped a donut, I'd laugh, tell them to toss it, and turn up the music. For the first time in a long time, culturally it was okay for people to make mistakes. It was okay for people to say they were stressed. We were all trying to do our best, and as long as we kept going and focused on the bigger picture, we'd get through anything.

#ADVERSITY

On April 7, 2020, less than a month after opening Square

Donut, I received a call that my mom was in the hospital. Nobody knew which hospital, only that she had been unconscious and taken from her home by ambulance. I frantically called every hospital in Omaha. I finally found where she was taken and learned she had immediately been placed on a ventilator after resuscitation. She had existing health problems and developed blood clots on her lungs, unrelated to Covid-19, for which they repeatedly tested her. Because of pandemic restrictions, I wasn't allowed to visit her in the hospital and had to wait for phone calls from doctors and nurses with progress reports. My mom is a strong person, so I assumed she'd be out of the hospital within a few weeks. At one point the doctors tried removing the ventilator only to put it back in.

It soon became clear that my mom wasn't going to recover quickly. After two failed attempts at removing her from the ventilator, the doctors said if she didn't start to show signs of improvement, the next step would be a tracheotomy. That spurred me to ask the nurses to let me talk to my mom on the phone by holding it to her ear. Most of them were hesitant because they believed it wouldn't do any good—she was sedated, on a paralytic medication, and couldn't hear me. They were also short staffed from the pandemic. I finally found one nurse, Sabrina, who agreed to put the phone to my mom's ear and leave it there for 15 minutes while I talked. Every time Sabrina had a night shift, she helped me talk to my mom on the phone. I spoke to my mom like I was in the room with her.

"I know you're scared, but I'm here, and I need you to get better."

"I'm still here, and I need you to keep fighting."

"We need you to respond and communicate with the doctors and nurses."

"Show me a sign you can hear me."

My mom is Catholic and comes from a strong line of deep believers who began intense prayer chains. They gave me specific prayers to recite, which I did every night.

My mom's favorite song is "Billie Jean" by Michael Jackson. One night, I told Jack and Maddie we needed to talk to Grandma on the phone together. After we all spoke to her, we played her song. When the song finished, Sabrina said my mom moved her hand while the song played. Shortly after that sign from my mother, the doctors wanted to try taking her off the ventilator again. The two previous attempts had failed because she experienced so much agitation and aggression—a common side effect patients experience after being on a ventilator for a prolonged period. I knew deep in my heart that if I could be with her while it was removed, I'd be able to help her get through the agitation. The doctors said it wasn't possible for me to be present because of Covid-19 restrictions. I promised them it would work if I was by her side and asked them to trust me. I knew if I was present, she would know and hear a familiar voice and I could talk her through it. I had to convince the doctors this might be the only way to finally remove the ventilator and avoid a tracheotomy.

A few days later, after clearing it with the doctors, they gave me permission and scheduled the procedure. When I arrived at the hospital and saw my mom for the first time in months, I was shocked at the sight of her. She had lost so much weight and looked so sick and frail. I held her hand in mine and bent over so my lips were right by her ear.

"You're going to breathe, stay calm, and it's going to be okay."

I didn't stop talking to her, repeating the same sentence. When the doctors removed the ventilator, she started to get aggressive. I continued to hold her hand, lean over her with my lips to her ear and soothe her, sometimes even getting stern and telling her to settle down. I felt our roles had officially switched and that I needed to speak to her as a parent. We repeated that cycle for hours, and the length of time between her agitated episodes increased. When it was time for me to leave that day, I begged the overnight nurse to continue to stay with her and talk to her as much as she could. When the doctor called me the next day, he said he was still unsure whether she'd remain off the ventilator, and if she went back on once more, she most likely wouldn't come off. I continued calling her room and asking the nurses to hold the phone to her ear.

Not only did my mom remain off the ventilator, but after

two long months she was transferred from the hospital to a rehab center where I could regularly visit. Unfortunately, she had suffered mental trauma and experienced bouts of dementia caused by the medications taken while hospitalized. Even though she survived, I felt like I had lost her. It was mentally and emotionally painful and exhausting. One night I needed sleep so badly, I turned off my phone. When I woke the next morning, my phone was flooded with texts and voice messages from the rehab center. My mom had experienced an episode during the night and was back in the hospital on a ventilator. I placed blame on myself for not being there for her. It was my fault for turning off my phone. The guilt felt insurmountable.

My mom's physician explained that being on a ventilator for a third time made chances for recovery slim. She asked if I had prepared for that possible outcome. I understood the message. That doctor was so compassionate and gentle with her words, but she was also truthful, and I respected that. However, I was numb and in denial. For reasons unexplained and miraculous, two days later, the doctors called and announced the ventilator had been removed and she was returning to rehab. Nobody could believe it, including the paramedics who had transported her to the hospital only two nights before. She still wasn't herself, but she began the slow road to recovery. On July 24th, 2020, she finally returned home with a detailed care plan requiring lots of support and supervision. I helped where I could with groceries, arranging for cleaning, and taking her to and from doctor appointments.

Although she no longer drives, her recovery has been amazing and the very definition of determination. I had a big task in front of me as her primary caretaker. I had to navigate supporting her while trying to operate a new business, all from survival mode. If not for the help of my cousins and extended family, my mom's recovery might have taken a different path, but she never gave up. She still relies on me and our extended family for transportation, groceries, and overseeing medical care.

#Disaster

When it rains it pours, and adversity usually happens when life is at its busiest. In June 2020, during the pandemic and my mother's hospitalization, disaster struck. My son had just finished an overnight shift making donuts and went home at 8am to sleep. I had just arrived at the shop to relieve him when he called.

"Mom, the house is on fire!"

At first, I didn't believe him.

"The house is on fire! Get home, now!"

The second time he said it, I realized he was serious. I ran out of the shop and sped home—a five-minute drive. I rounded the corner to my street, nearly tipping my car, and pulled up to my house. Thick smoke spilled out of the front office windows, but there were no firefighters in sight. My son stood in the driveway with people I didn't recognize except for my neighbor who held a fire extinguisher in his hand and looked at me with such sympathy, I cried.

My son quickly explained that he'd been upstairs in his bedroom when he heard glass shatter. He opened his bedroom door and immediately faced smoke and intense heat. He slammed the door but realized it was his only way out. He grabbed a shirt, covered his face, and ran downstairs and out the front door. Within minutes, a group of men descended onto the property. They were construction workers from a nearby site and while on a crane, one of them witnessed an explosion at our house. The men abandoned their equipment and sprinted through yards, jumping fences to reach my house.

Jack realized that our dog, Fly, was still inside, and without hesitation, one worker ran inside. He found her, and even though she bit him out of fear, he grabbed and rescued her. Another worker pulled my garden hose inside to try and put out the fire, which was primarily contained in the front office. He noticed piles of paperwork, my laptop, and photos on the desk and positioned himself between those items and the flames in an effort to save it all, which he did. I was able to preserve photos of the Pooley farm, the paperwork for my mom's healthcare, and my work laptop. The men continued to fight the fire until the fire department arrived, 15 minutes after I did. My property is positioned oddly in the subdivision, and the firefighters couldn't easily find it.

The firefighters took over, and I hugged each construction worker and thanked them through my tears. I asked for their names, but they said they didn't want any special recognition. A few days later, I drove to that construction site and brought them breakfast as a thank you and invited their families to enjoy free donuts any time, but to my knowledge, I never saw any of them again.

The cause of the fire was a large garden pot on the front porch. The year before, I had started a planting project and filled the pot with peat moss. I intended to add a fertilizer mix to the moss but hadn't done it, and the bag of granulated fertilizer sat on top of the moss for months. The combination of winter freeze followed by intense summer heat plus that morning's strong breeze created the perfect condition for the pot to ignite and explode.

The fire destroyed the entire east side of the house, and coupled with the smoke damage, the fire marshal deemed it unsafe to stay. My insurance company found us a hotel, where we stayed for the next few weeks until temporary housing was arranged. We eventually moved into an apartment, but it was difficult to find comfort anywhere with my life in pieces. I turned the hotel room closet into an office and continued to operate in survival mode. At times I didn't know whether to work on the business, my mom's healthcare paperwork, or home repair and insurance issues.

Even with that much upheaval in my life, I didn't stop to ask, "Why me?" I had to keep going, afraid that if I stopped, I would have to face a reality I didn't want to acknowledge. I had to let go of small details, such as worrying about if every donut was perfectly square. Determination—and lots of it—was the only thing that got me through those challenging months.

#Loss

The fire was hard on everyone, including our dog Fly, a 17-year-old miniature Australian Shepherd. She had struggled when we moved from the farm into a residential house, and the move to a hotel and then an apartment after the fire was even worse. Her health declined, and I felt helpless. In November 2020, the insurance company stopped paying for our apartment, so Jack, Fly, and I moved back into the house even though repairs weren't finished. Flooring hadn't been installed, it hadn't been painted, furniture was still in storage, and none of the interior doors had been hung. I put butcher paper over the windows because we had no window coverings. I put blankets on the sub-flooring so Fly had a place to lie down. It was a skeleton of a home and we lived out of boxes and suitcases for several months.

Over the next month, Fly's health continued to fail. She could no longer walk outside to the grass, so I had to carry her and set her down each time. I knew that year would be

Three Pints Determination

her last Christmas, and between the tears of that thought and the unfinished state of the house, I didn't bother to put up a Christmas tree. After suffering a fall and starting to urinate in her sleep, in March 2021, we made the difficult decision to euthanize her. We buried her on the 15 acres of farmland that my ex-husband still owned, and though it was painful to let her go, I knew it was for the best. It still hurts to this day.

After Fly's death, the weight of the loss I experienced over that year became too much. I felt like I wasn't in control of my business, my house was not a home, my mom wasn't back to being my mom, and my beloved dog was gone. I felt displaced, and the only familiar place that offered comfort was my car. I took many drives during that time and sat in my car and cried, laughed, and even ate a few meals. I didn't want to burden my kids with my stress even though they knew I was struggling, and I didn't want to continually burden my friends with the weight of what I was going through. Only God knew, and I relied heavily on my faith.

One of the best decisions I made during that time was to give up—not give up on my business or life, but to let go. I turned my life over to God and changed my perspective. At the shop, instead of worrying that the donut icing was short of the proofing line, I was grateful the donuts were iced. At home, instead of complaining how the lawn was cut, I was happy it was mowed. Instead of spending my time with my mom buying groceries and running errands, we spent more time talking. The greatest growth and change occurs when you're at your lowest point.

Ingredient tip: Add Determination While Constantly Stirring

When life is at its worst, it is tempting to give up and look for an easy way out. But those are the times when you need to dig in deep. The resilience inside you—determination—gets you through adversity to keep driving forward. You might need to pause and look for ways to make time for yourself, but life doesn't stop and neither should you. I compare myself to one of those inflatable clowns with sand in the bottom—no matter how many times you knock it down, it pops back up. The only way you'll reach a place of success and happiness is if you have a steady source of determination driving you toward your dreams.

4

FOUR QUARTS LEADERSHIP

No matter the dream you're trying to achieve, you'll need to become an effective leader. The right leadership style matters—you need to find a healthy balance between sincerity and authority. Operating too heavily in one direction or the other will inhibit growth both professionally and personally. Strong leadership ensures your success, helps you win, and ultimately brings you happiness.

#NewChallenges

With my mom's recovery in progress, having moved back into my house, and having mourned the loss of Fly, I was finally able to focus on a new year. The business began to regulate, and I breathed a little easier. Unfortunately, that didn't last long. In April 2021, several staff issues occurred simultaneously. Three of my cashiers came down with Covid-19. My head baker suffered a hernia during off-work hours and had to change careers because he could no longer meet the lifting requirements.

Flexibility is key as an employee at a start-up company, and some people are better suited to a more predictable, stable work environment. My assistant baker was one of those people. He had been struggling with the constant changes, so he resigned without knowing the head baker had also just resigned. Forty-eight hours later, another employee I was training to become head decorator told me she was leaving to move out of state for family reasons. My fryer had been showing signs that he was unhappy in his job—he seemed overly tired and slow to perform. Although he was trying to work hard, his capacity to do so had diminished. I knew he was afraid of disappointing me, but I recognized his exhaustion and knew he wasn't happy in the position. We had an open, honest conversation and agreed it would be best for him to leave once he found another position and I had hired a new fryer.

With over 75 percent of my employees out and getting news that I had been turned down for three Covid-19 relief programs due to the untimely start of my business, I was at an impasse. Logistically, I couldn't operate, so I cut the head off the snake and decided to close for the month of May. I knew it was better to close for 30 days and focus on preventing future closures than stay open and simply put a bandage on a larger problem. I couldn't afford to take such a financial hit, nor could I operate with a skeleton staff. Luckily, my remaining employees were in financial positions where they all said they wouldn't be impacted by lack of payment for those 30 days. My head decorator was the only salaried employee, and I did continue to pay him during that time. I also made a gut-wrenching, brutally honest post on social media about the closure. It was the most viewed post we'd ever had with more than 900 likes and 110 comments of support.

During the closure, I took the opportunity to replace lost staff. I posted all job positions, but out of dozens of interviews scheduled, only three people showed. This was no surprise, because in the past I'd had over 110 interviews scheduled over the course of three months with only a handful of applicants who showed up. It wasn't just me—the hiring shortage was universal. In fact, a local TV station contacted me about a story they were doing on staffing shortages. This was my opportunity to capitalize in hopes of getting more applicant exposure. I agreed to be interviewed, and after the story aired, I received an influx of applicants who actually showed up for the interviews. I was able to hire two bakers, two fryers, a decorator, and additional cashiers. Most of them had little to no experience, which I preferred. I was able to train them in the manner I wanted and reopened the shop on June 1, 2021.

. . .

#S‍tep‍U‍p

Training an almost entirely new staff represented a turning point in many ways. I no longer had to fill in for vacant shifts throughout the shop, which resulted in a change in my leadership style. Prior to that point, it was all hands on deck, and I regularly worked alongside the bakers, decorators, and cashiers, becoming a co-worker rather than a boss. Staff shared personal stories with me, and I was quick to help whenever I could, whether that meant slipping someone $20 to buy food or granting extra time off for personal reasons. I also fixed staff mistakes rather than take the time to let them address their own mistakes. I was in a position where I couldn't afford to have anyone leave, so I ignored boundaries, which prevented the business and the employees from experiencing growth.

As I began to run the business instead of working it, the business improved, so I began to implement necessary changes to hold staff accountable, allowing me to focus more on the business. I was met with a lot of resistance from staff. They were upset that I was no longer "one of them" because I reestablished my role as boss and business owner, no longer allowing them to take advantage of my desire to help. Many of them struggled with that change, so hiring new staff was the perfect time for me to step up. Mutual trust and respect come from empowering employees to do their job and make mistakes as well as succeed. Empowering an employee may even be in the form of moving them to a different role. When their perspective changes, their priorities change, which better sets them up for success. Business owners either buy themselves a job or buy themselves a business. Owners who maintain an equal role with employees simply bought themselves a job, but those who train employees to lead bought themselves a business.

My improved leadership style worked well with the new staff. I trusted them to do their jobs, and they respected my boundaries as an owner. I was able to spend more time in a supportive role for employees and engage with customers, and business steadily grew into 2022. In January of that year, my head baker left his shift one night and hit a deer while driving home. He broke his collarbone and couldn't work for three months.

Suddenly, I was back to working 16-hour days in the shop, once again a peer instead of a boss. The back-of-house staff started to rely on me as a security blanket whenever something went wrong because I was right there to step in and fix it. The front-of-house staff had been well-trained and was able to function without me, but I was no longer available to provide the type of leadership and support they needed. I also didn't have the ability to engage with customers. I focused solely on the back of the house and maintaining donut production. Marketing, accounting, and administrative tasks took a back seat as well. Slowly, sales decreased, and employees grew tired and frustrated.

When my head baker returned to work on a limited basis in April 2022, he also had a period of weight restrictions. Within another month, he was back to full capacity, and I took the opportunity to pull back from the kitchen. This enabled me to once again be the boss and provide all employees with leadership-level support as well as engage with customers. It also reinforced the need to maintain a healthy boundary between boss and employee. A boss doesn't need to be a peer to show employees they care; they simply need to exhibit sincerity and inclusion. Patience, empathy, and communication are the qualities needed for sincere interaction. Asking questions, listening, and understanding establish mutual trust and respect. Treating your employees like family is important, but families need to have boundaries. A good business owner can navigate the nuances of employee communication. There are appropriate times to invite discussion and there are times when decisions are simply made. When you step back from working "in" the business and are able to work "on" the business, that's when your employees flourish, gain confidence, and feel their value increase. It's also when the business starts to grow, and that's a win.

Leadership also extends outside your business into your community and industry. I was active on social media and posted photos of our unique products: donuts of the month, donuts shaped as letters, and specialty decorated donuts. Soon, a few local donut shops started producing similar products. At first, I was angry—I had worked so hard to create this new landscape for the industry and didn't want others stealing my ideas. Then I remembered imitation is the best form of flattery. Other donut shops across the nation started to follow us on social media. I learned that a competing grocery chain bakery much bigger than Square Donut held management meetings about us. It gave me confidence and validated that we were on the right track and had become a leader in the industry.

Ingredient Tip: Let it Rise

Leadership comes in many forms and can go through periods of rising and falling. It's important to recognize when your leadership style is working and when it isn't. Good leadership exhibits patience, empathy, and communication while maintaining boundaries. Empowering those around you to succeed leads to mutual growth, happiness, and success in your business.

5

FIVE DASHES GRACE

*E*veryone makes mistakes. How you react to those mistakes will impact your ability to be successful. When something goes wrong, do you dwell on it? Do you become paralyzed and unable to function? Do you hold back because you're afraid to make another mistake? Maybe you're the opposite extreme where you work so hard you don't allow yourself any flexibility or room to grow. Giving yourself grace in those difficult moments will help propel you toward your goals and ultimately your dream.

#Perfectionism

While in the throes of filling in for my head baker, I became hyper-focused on perfectionism. A donut didn't leave the kitchen unless the icing was exactly to the proofing line or the sprinkles were distributed evenly. I answered every text and email even if it meant responding in the middle of the night. I felt compelled to explain my actions and defend my decisions. If a customer was upset, I carried it with me for days. My relentless pursuit of perfectionism turned into 100-hour work weeks. I wasn't sleeping or eating right. Twice I found myself so dehydrated and exhausted that I ended up in the ER on an IV for fluids and rest. Debilitating perfectionism was literally killing me.

I couldn't snap my fingers and stop being a perfectionist, but I could move from debilitating perfectionism to productive perfectionism. I had a great staff in place so there was no reason to avoid stepping away from work. In fact, that was the only way the business would grow in the manner I needed it to. Making that conscious choice to let go was enlightening. Allowing myself grace was like waking up in the morning with a new pair of glasses and a whole new perspective. I started practicing productive perfectionism with the donuts. If the sprinkles were uneven every now and then, I let it go. If the chocolate icing was a little bubbly on a donut, it was okay. As long as a flaw wasn't chronic, I wasn't going to stress. I learned to embrace the artisan aspect of donuts, flaws and all. I also learned how to prioritize—a phone call from my mother was more important than answering a bunch of work texts. If I lost out on an order because I didn't immediately open the email, I had to come to terms with it.

Productive perfectionism doesn't mean a lack of focus or acceptance of mediocracy. It means giving yourself grace to accept that you're human. It also means you recognize your value and have the confidence to protect it. Now, when I need to leave work for personal reasons, I don't explain where I'm going. Instead, I let staff know that I'm leaving and what time I'll return. If a customer is waiting, rather than apologize I thank them for their patience. If an employee needs to talk, I let them know I have 10 minutes and if we're not finished in that time, I offer to continue the discussion later—I'm still practicing that skill. By modeling productive perfectionism and granting myself grace, I've taught the staff to do the same, which has resulted in better communication, respect, and trust across the board.

#DontSkipSteps

Because many entrepreneurs are perfectionists, it's easy for that perfectionism to quickly become debilitating. If you're having a difficult time moving to productive perfectionism and giving yourself grace, start by making a simple list of steps to follow and commit to completing them, even if something else doesn't get done. When I sit down to answer an email, I address it in its entirety and ignore distractions. If I must measure a space for a piece of equipment, I don't put it off because I have five other things on my to do list. If I'm placing an order and realize I'm going to be late to an appointment, rather than rush through the order, I finish and let my appointment know I'll be 5 minutes late. When I want to promote an employee, rather than rush them into the position because I need someone, I have them spend time in other roles—washing dishes or baking—so they understand multiple aspects of the business. When you're operating in a state of debilitating perfectionism, you don't take the time to complete steps because you want everything done at once. But what happens is that instead of taking the time now—even if it's harder—you end up paying for it later.

Not skipping steps is important not only in your personal and professional life but also in your spiritual life. One of the first things I lost when operating from a place of debilitating perfectionism was my relationship with God. Skipping steps with Him made my life harder. I became ungrateful and it manifested in negative ways. When I take the time to make God a priority, I feel less stressed and more confident because instead of carrying my burdens, I give them to Him. Rather than stressing over mistakes or unfinished business, I follow the steps to give thanks—I pause, meditate, enjoy nature, or drink a cup of coffee on my swing. Making the change to productive perfectionism and giving myself grace was one of the most difficult changes I've made, and I struggle with it daily. But by staying on task and not skipping steps, I've enabled my business and myself to grow beyond measure.

Ingredient Tip: A Little Grace Goes a Long Way

You don't have to be perfect to be successful. People learn and grow through their mistakes. Mistakes are lessons. Allowing yourself grace will help you develop confidence, recognize your value, and trust your actions. Letting go of things isn't a sign of weakness or lack of capability. Giving up control shows that you trust the process and those surrounding you. Going back to basics and not skipping steps now will save time, stress, and unnecessary mistakes, as well as help you grow personally, professionally, and spiritually so that you can achieve your dreams.

6

SIX TABLESPOONS SELF-CARE

Without your health, you have nothing. Self-care has become a more public topic in the last few years for good reason: It's easy to ignore your physical and mental needs when you're stressed, constantly working, and on the go. But you can't take care of others—or a business—if you aren't taking care of yourself. If self-care is left unattended, nature will find an unwelcome way to take care of it for you.

#FeelingGood

When a business makes it to its fourth or fifth year, things really start rolling. Standards are established, processes flow, and every piece falls into place. It was when Pooley's Pumpkin Patch reached that point that I was at my best regarding self-care. The business was successful and self-sustaining, so I felt I could afford downtime. Every morning and evening, I found a private outdoor spot on the farm where I sat, surrounded by nature. I took daily solo walks. I went to the gym three times a week. I ate whole, healthy foods, including vegetables from our garden. I was in a peaceful place spiritually. I had time to create visions for the business and able to work at my own pace and focus on things of my choosing. I was able to be present in my kids' lives, in my business, and with my health.

Despite my divorce, closing the pumpkin patch, and working a desk job, I was motivated by the thought of starting another business. Innovation excites me, and prior to opening Square Donut, I was physically in a good place. I was an empty nester and ready for my next purpose in life. Even though the nine months prior to Square Donut's soft opening were busy and full of challenges, I was excited for the next chapter.

#**SlowDecline**

My self-care first started to fail at the onset of the pandemic. During my mom's hospitalization, it was tough keeping up with the initial changes to the business while caring for her. Then, the house fire increased my stress exponentially. I no longer had a home that offered a respite, so I poured myself into work. I spent longer hours at the shop, trying to control my professional life because my personal life felt out of control. My stress level was like an interest rate that compounded every 30 days.

Mentally, I tried to stay positive, leaning heavily on my faith. But my physical health declined. I didn't take daily walks like I had done at the farm. I didn't want to cook in the temporary apartment, so I ate fast food. I wasn't in my own bed, so I didn't sleep well at night. However, I also didn't feel like I had a choice—it was either live that lifestyle or let the business go bankrupt and give up. Instead of admitting I was going down an unhealthy path, I focused on my goals and worked even harder. I told myself it was all temporary. As soon as my mom recovered and my home repairs were finished, I'd prioritize my health, but in the meantime, I pretended I was invincible.

When my mom was finally out of the woods and I moved back into my house, rather than resume my self-care, I was mentally and physically exhausted. I overate because it "felt good." I laid on the couch and watched mindless TV because I couldn't decompress enough to find a balance. I had gone so long without a haircut, I convinced myself it wouldn't hurt to wait a little longer. I barely had the energy to keep up with work let alone maintain my health.

Just when I thought the worst was behind me, the staff challenges occurred, and I closed Square Donut for a month. The first thing I did was sleep, but I didn't allow myself any other "luxuries." Instead, I got right back to work interviewing, hiring, and training new staff. I returned to long work hours, telling myself it was progress, and once I got through the 3-month training process, I could breathe again and develop a better routine and schedule.

By fall 2021, the business was finally sustaining. I no longer received phone calls in the middle of the night with questions from the baker, and I slept until 4am with some regularity. I started cooking a little at home again and realized how much better it made me feel. But I hesitated to launch into a self-care routine. It had taken months until I wasn't constantly exhausted, and I didn't want to start something if I couldn't be consistent. I wanted to be in a better place physically and mentally before I recommitted to regular self-care. I was also waiting for another shoe to drop.

#RockBottom

Not only did I continue to neglect my health, but it continued to decline after my head baker's accident. This time, because I personally assumed the role of head baker, I worked 18-hour days, seven days a week. I thought about hiring a temporary baker, but it would take them three to four months to get up to speed, which was the same length of time as my head baker's recovery. I knew it was a risk to assume he would return, but I decided to stay committed to him. It also gave me a chance to show my commitment to the rest of the staff by getting my hands dirty in the kitchen while ensuring our procedures and efficiencies were met. Those were my goals.

For the next three months, my typical day began when I arrived at the shop at 5am. I spent the first six hours on administrative tasks: emails, phone messages, payroll, marketing, and ordering supplies. At 11am I made the daily dough sheet, which listed how much dough to prep, the number of each product, and any custom orders. At 1pm I'd close out the register from that morning's sales. After staff left, I'd spend another two or three hours on additional work, and then leave at 4 or 5pm to complete the daily bank deposit. Then I'd go home, eat dinner—usually fast food—and return to work at 7pm where as head baker I'd make the dough, cut it, fry it, and help with a portion of the side work, including dishes. I'd return home at 3am, shower, sleep for a few hours, and then return to work.

I tried to see my mother once a week and help her when I could, but I was careful not to confide in her how much I was struggling physically and mentally. In fact, I was careful not to let anyone see it. I made sure to always put a smile on my face and tell everyone that I was fine. The staff didn't know the severity of the situation. The morning employees didn't see me coming in at night, and vice versa with the overnight employees. My son Jack, who helped me with the business, knew I was working a lot of hours, as was he, and he worried about me. But he was also running his own side business, so even he didn't see the full extent of it. He'd try to help by ordering groceries to have delivered to the house, but nobody could truly help if I wasn't willing to be honest.

By March 2022, the physical stress had turned into a health crisis. I started forgetting to pay bills, I'd store the milk in a cabinet instead of the refrigerator, and I couldn't remember conversations. I'd get uncontrollably angry or cry over the smallest things. One night, I was so physically exhausted, I couldn't walk and crawled up the stairs to my bedroom. Desperate for help, twice that month I drove to the ER, where they administered IV fluids and provided a place to rest for a few hours. I didn't tell a single person about those instances—if I did, I knew they'd pressure me to slow down and work less, and I felt I couldn't make that change. It was as if I had made a deal with the devil: Square Donut would be my legacy, but I would die doing it. I was so sure a heart attack was inevitable, I contacted my attorney to get my legal affairs in order so I'd have a plan in place for my children. I even wrote them both letters to read when I was gone.

In April 2022, I had an episode where I couldn't breathe and had excruciating back pain on one side of my body. Assuming I had somehow broken a rib, I asked Jack to drive me to the after-hours clinic. A female physician performed a full checkup, diagnosing the back pain as tight muscle spasms from stress. She asked questions about my lifestyle, and I felt comfortable confiding in her. I told her about my business and personal life and how difficult it had been. She empathized and told me she had several friends who were business owners and understood the tendency to hide the truth from people about the difficulties business owners face, the long hours they work, and the stress that resulted. She prescribed muscle relaxers for my back and instructed me to go straight home and rest, no exceptions. The physician was firm but honest when she ended the visit by saying I could take her advice or ignore it, but if I ignored it, she would see me back in the ER for a much more serious condition. I took her advice to heart.

Jack drove me home, and I only told him that my back was in spasm—I didn't tell him the extent of what the doctor said. When I got home, I took a shower and broke down, bawling. I knew I couldn't keep going at the rate I had been. There's a misconception that if you appear okay on the outside, you're fine on the inside. I had pretended to be "strong" for too long. I felt like I was in Hell, and I prayed for God to take over. If I was going to live, I needed to stop making excuses.

#KeepItSimple

Change is never easy, especially when it affects your physical and mental health. The first thing I had to do was implement boundaries in all areas of my life. One of my biggest problem areas was lack of sleep, so I started by making a commitment to sleep longer and not go into the shop until 8:30am. Even on days when the kitchen was short-staffed, I told the team to do the best they could without me. It was hard not to swoop in and fill the gap, but they had the experience to handle things without me.

I also established boundaries in my personal life. On the days I helped my mother, rather than spend the entire time working through her to-do lists, I spent the time sitting and visiting with her, something we both needed. I only answered calls when I felt mentally prepared to talk, and I quit feeling guilty when I didn't answer. I set boundaries with people who thought I was merely being stubborn because I didn't want to go out and who didn't realize I was protecting my personal time. I also accepted the fact I needed help and didn't worry about spending money to preserve my physical and mental well-being. I hired a cleaning service, had my groceries delivered, and made a list of the unfinished house renovations, such as painting rooms and finishing the deck. I also let Jack help more at home, which was difficult because I had always been able to do those tasks myself, but now couldn't.

I slowly added other small, simple steps—steps that I didn't skip and could follow most of the time. My meals had been both unhealthy and erratic, so I committed to eating a healthy breakfast every morning. I knew I couldn't yet commit to three healthy meals every day, but I could focus on one. I also started taking my vitamins every morning—another way to improve my health from the inside out.

Starting small and building upon a good foundation is the only way to ensure you don't skip steps. If you start with big goals, you set yourself up to fail. One of the best exercises I often apply both personally and professionally is from the book *The 5 Second Rule* by Mel Robbins:

> "The moment you have an instinct to act on a goal, you must physically move within 5 seconds or your brain will kill it. When you feel yourself hesitate before doing something that you know you should do, count 5-4-3-2-1 GO and move towards action."

This exercise has helped tremendously with my self-care. For example, if I'm running late and start to tell myself I'll take my vitamins later, I stop, count 5-4-3-2-1, and take my vitamins. Not only does it help me act, but it reminds me to put myself first, free of any pressure or guilt when doing so. It allows me to take the time to complete steps, which is necessary for recovery and growth.

Considering the physical and mental condition I was in, I'd currently give myself a grade of "C" regarding self-care. I'm not perfect every day, but I am getting eight hours of sleep most days and not skipping the commitments I've made. Every morning upon waking, I spend two minutes stretching, breathing, and looking out the window at nature in peaceful meditation. I haven't resumed regular exercise like daily walks because I'm not at a point where I'm confident I won't skip that step. But I know I will add it when the time is right and I can commit to it. It might take months, a year, or more until I'm ready, but everyone is on a different timeline. For now, when I'm tired, I sleep and when I'm hungry, I eat. I can at least look in the mirror and know that I'm trying.

Ingredient Tip: Sprinkle in Plenty of Self-care

Nothing is worth sacrificing your physical and mental health. It can slip away quickly and be easy to ignore. You must be willing to put yourself before anyone or anything else. As a business owner, always put your own well-being before your business, even if that means a bad review because you had to close for a day for personal reasons. You must practice regular self-care and build up a good foundation so that you establish strong habits and commit to them. Let go of perfectionism, control, and the fear of not being seen as "strong" or "put together." Don't put off self-care for a later time—the time for self-care is now.

7

SEVEN TEASPOONS OPTIMISM

Some people are naturally optimistic and always have a positive outlook on life. For others, it can be difficult to remain optimistic, especially during times of adversity. It's also hard to stay positive when the future is unknown. But optimistic people trust that no matter what happens, they are ultimately responsible for achieving their dreams by finding their own version of happiness and success.

#**Positive**

In chapter one I shared that I always strive to create a happy Norman Rockwell type of environment for myself and others. This desire is the result of a traumatic childhood in which I used optimism as a coping mechanism. As an adult, it's because I know a negative attitude leads to negative results both physically and mentally, and I don't need to add to life's challenges.

I've been told many times throughout my life that I wasn't good enough—the teacher who told me I was stupid, or acquaintances who said my business ideas would never work. Those voices can be loud, but optimism is how I quiet them and stop my former tendencies toward self sabotage.

Optimism is how I remind myself that I'm capable, a fighter, and someone who goes after their dreams. Combining those characteristics with optimism is an unstoppable formula—how do you stop a determined, optimistic woman? The answer is you can't!

You have to practice optimism daily so that it becomes a habit and a core principle that you adopt in your life. I choose to see the positive in everything and perpetually try to find the good. That positivity starts with my meditation every morning. I even thank God in my prayers for the adversity in my life because it has made me a stronger person.

Sometimes that strength is for my own challenges and other times my strength has helped someone else. Optimism is contagious and should be role modeled. I make it a goal to show others that they can get through anything. When someone points out a problem, let them know everything will be okay and that you'll address it together. Help them find one good thing or one opportunity from that problem.

People who lack optimism tend to be dependent, which means they have insecurities about their own abilities, value, and worth. When I interview a potential employee who is dependent, it doesn't mean I don't hire them, it just means I'll have to help them more. I enjoy helping people develop their confidence and optimism. I do this by empowering them within their role as an employee. I give them room to make mistakes and show them that despite errors, everything will be okay and they can move forward. This helps build their confidence and self-esteem to overcome their insecurities and dependence.

Once I help them establish this independence, I work with them to develop interdependence. This trait is important because it means you must listen to others, work together, and express your own optimism when something goes wrong.

I had an employee who experienced a lot of anxiety at work. One day, leading up to a busy holiday, I knew she'd be especially nervous. I wrote her a note the day before, assuring her that everything would be okay and I knew she'd be able to manage and get through it. When I walked into the shop the next morning, she exemplified a calm employee who was in complete control. Just that little bit of optimism went a long way. I strive to use my optimism to help employees in at least one area—whether professionally or personally—that they can carry with them throughout life. To me, that's a huge success.

. . .

#**Future**

Square Donut will soon be entering its fourth year, and we've successfully hired a great staff and created the right processes. We're now in observation mode and defining what we want the business to look like and who we are as a brand. We're on track with our new product development and are ahead of the game—instead of reacting to everything, we can be proactive.

I'm optimistic that the worst is behind us and the best is yet to come. Because I'm finally engaging in self-care, my optimism is flowing freely. I'm at the stage where I can envision the business's growth and the possibilities for franchising. I'm also developing spin-offs for new businesses.

However, if the tide turned and I was faced with the decision to go back to 100-hour work weeks or sell the business, I would sell. Square Donut's growth has been incredible despite Covid-19, so I've already hit my mark for what I set out to accomplish.

Would I be disappointed if I didn't turn it into a franchise or million-dollar business? Probably, but that doesn't mean it isn't a success and it certainly doesn't mean I'd be giving up. It means that I have the experience and the wisdom to know what makes me happy and brings me peace. I see the value and worth in my health, especially for my kids. I trust God because I've faced adversity and come out on the other side. This makes me optimistic about the future.

One of the goals that excites me is passing on Square Donut to my son Jack who can help develop it into a corporate franchise. I'd love to have the current shop become the flagship location, with Square Donut franchises across the country. I'd also love to franchise other business opportunities. The visionary in me already has plans in motion for a new business venture that has come from what I've learned through Square Donut.

My talent is creating businesses, branding, marketing, and customer service—those have always been my strengths. I'm not locked in to one industry or business idea. For the first time in my life, I can start a business simply because it's what I enjoy, not because I lack emotional or financial security. That's such an exciting and comforting place to be.

Even though I'm still in the creative window, I know I can scale a new business and either sell it or turn it into a franchise so that any owner can run with it without being in the sink or swim position that I was. Whenever someone says they are scared to start a business, my first reaction is, "What are you scared of?" Whatever their answer, I follow by asking, "What can you do if what you're afraid of happens?" Solve that problem and then solve the next problem, and the next, until you realize you're afraid of something that may not even happen. But if it does, you've already thought through the solutions.

Their feeling of fear is normal, but I want them to realize that no obstacle is too big to overcome. I've been through a lot, and I'm no longer afraid. If you employ interdependent people, you can rely on them for help and problem solving. Even when they make mistakes, you know they will be able to move forward. This should help alleviate any fears and bring a sense of peace that everything will be okay.

Delegating the task of problem solving is one way you can bounce back from adversity. It's also a key element to a successful, profitable business with a healthy work-life balance within the post-Covid-19 environment. The new business landscape is a hybrid—gone are the days when business owners must sacrifice their personal lives. If managed correctly, a business should be scalable and sustainable. I want to help other business owners so they don't have to work as hard as I did. I want to inspire people and make a difference in the world. And I want to leave a legacy for my kids.

I've had business ideas in the past that sounded great on a personal level, but they weren't sustainable, so those ideas were tossed in the trash. Had it not been for Covid-19, Square Donut's profitability would have been the equivalent of its fifth year in business in only its third year.

Given a new business venture, I know I can achieve that level of profitability within the first three years. I'm proud of

Square Donut's success. I value the work I've put into it, the ideas we've incorporated, and its execution. I don't apologize for my success, and I don't apologize for my failures. I remain humble and focused on why I'm a business owner—I want to create a place where people can feel comfortable and happy.

#Vision

Action should follow optimism. It does no good to be optimistic if you aren't willing to put in the work. You can be optimistic about a new business venture, but you must properly operate that business and exhibit good leadership. All the sales in the world won't matter if you don't have the right team in place and can show them good leadership.

I'm sure you've known business owners who were ruthless and even cruel, as well as others who were pushovers who let people take advantage of them. The most successful business owners have patience, empathy, and can communicate while also establishing boundaries.

Optimism is contagious, especially in the workplace. I've experienced firsthand how optimism helps an employee grow and improve in their role and as a person. When I share my optimism with my staff, I witness them sharing their own optimism with customers.

I've also experienced it within myself. Time and time again when I've been down or have negative thoughts, I reframe my thinking and verbalize positive thoughts. "I may be down now, but not for long!" It might not always look like what I envisioned, but optimism helps me to think bigger so that my actions follow suit. You can be anything you want to be, so why not think big!

When opportunities arise, an optimist acts because they have a strong vision for the future. For some, that future might involve making a certain amount of money. Although money can't bring you happiness, it can provide security so you can focus on the things that make you happy.

When I have financial security, I enjoy using money to help others, especially through non-profit organizations. I also use it to establish a foundation for my kids so they don't have to endure the extreme financial and emotional insecurities that I've experienced. If I can provide them with a certain level of stability, it frees them to make decisions that fit their own vision for peace and happiness.

My vision represents the feelings of peace and security I lacked growing up. My goal is to create my Norman Rockwell painting: an acreage where I can take daily walks, a warm, welcoming home with a big fireplace I can sit by, chickens and goats roaming the property, and an outdoor swing where I can sip my coffee every morning.

My vision also includes travel and embracing life. Everything I'm doing now helps me get one step closer to achieving that dream, and optimism is the thread that connects it all together.

Ingredient tip: Mix Optimism until Bubbly

Optimism is one of the greatest weapons against fear, insecurity, and inaction. Even when you don't know the outcome, optimism drives you to act anyway. It also serves as a reminder that you can get through any challenge. Good leaders exemplify optimism and know that it has a trickle-down effect. It is a thread that connects your decisions and provides the vision for peace, happiness, and culmination of your dreams.

8

EIGHT OUNCES WISDOM

Wisdom is a gift meant to be shared. Your experiences provide you with a unique knowledge base. You can share your wisdom in many ways—with your employees, friends, family, and community, whether as an employer, advisor, or mentor. You'll always be most remembered for how you treat others.

#AWARENESS

The way you gain wisdom is through experience. Another piece of advice I can give to any new business owner is to spend time in every role for which you plan to hire employees. It's critical that you understand every detail of your business, inside and out. This understanding is part of not skipping steps, discussed in chapter five. I could easily have skipped washing dishes at the donut shop and assume I knew how to do that job, but I didn't want to skip a single step in understanding my business and establishing its processes. Spending time in each position—baking, decorating, cashiering, receiving—also helped me write job descriptions when I needed to hire and train for those roles. It was only by experiencing each position firsthand that I was able to have the knowledge needed to share with my employees.

Hiring is one area in which I've gained extensive experience over the last three years. Startups are unique in that processes can quickly change from one day to the next, so success depends on hiring the right type of person. The ideal startup employee is secure, has very little ego, and able to handle constructive criticism. Just when you've done something one way, the owner might tell you to change it and walk away. The employee must be able to make the change without overthinking it. Of all the people I've hired at Square Donut over the last three years, only about 12 percent possessed those qualities. But now I know the right questions to ask and what to listen for during interviews.

When you don't skip steps and spend time in each role within your business, you can ask the right questions during an interview to make sure the person you hire is a good fit for the role. I often feel like a psychologist during an interview, trying to uncover a candidate's true personality. During an interview, if I ask a candidate, "Are you flexible and able to quickly adapt to a changing work environment?" they will answer yes because they want the job. But if I ask, "If you build a house, would you insist on having a formal dining room?" some candidates will answer "no" and others will answer "yes." If they insist on having a formal dining room, it tells me they may not adapt to change easily, but they are probably good at following procedures. If they don't insist on having a formal dining room, it tells me they are flexible, but I need to dig deeper to find out if they are too laid back for the role. Continuing to ask creative questions reveals a lot about the prospective employees and if they'll fit in with the team you're trying to build.

When I was in survival mode during Covid-19, I was desperate for employees and not as discerning as I should have been when hiring. That behavior resulted in some toxic hires. A colleague shared this advice: "Hire slowly and fire quickly." This bit of wisdom has been invaluable. If you hire an employee who isn't a match for your business or your team, the best thing you can do is to quickly let them go and not let the problem linger. I've also learned it's best to take your time when hiring. One of my employees was very quiet during the interview and didn't convey much energy. At first, I was unsure how they'd do in the fast, high-energy environment at Square Donut. But during the interview process, after asking more questions, I was able to determine they were a strong person, so I hired them. The employee has turned out to be a calming presence during times of chaos.

They are direct but professional and have the ability to recognize other employees' strengths and weaknesses.

During another interview, I was hiring for a baker. The candidate was young and inexperienced, which meant I could train him in a specific way and help him grow into the position. However, there was also the risk that after teaching him everything I knew, he would leave and go to a competitor. Based on what I learned during the interview, I was willing to take that risk because if he stayed, it meant production would improve, profits would increase, his wage would increase, he'd receive benefits, and he would stay long-term. Training him took longer than expected, but it was worth it in the end. Finding the right team isn't just about who fits the skill set; it's about finding a team that gels and works toward the greater good. I've gone through a lot of employees because most can't handle the rapid changes that happen within my business, but the ones who stay have become very close and share mutual trust and respect.

#Honesty

I believe in treating others the way you want to be treated, whether it's an employee, customer, friend, or family member. This belief is why I value sincerity and authenticity in my employees. There's a time and place in business to care about dollar signs, but when it comes to employees, I try to show them I care through my actions and my honesty. If I see that an employee isn't happy in their job, I don't want them to stay out of obligation or because it's a paycheck. If someone works the night shift but is miserable, it will eventually affect their quality of work. I have no problem talking to an employee and pointing out that I think they aren't happy in their position. They are usually relieved, which leads to a larger conversation about their goals. I once hired a cashier who was a great individual but not a people person. In fact, interacting with customers all day brought out the worst in her, and I had to let her go. She was always very thorough with her side work and cleaning, so during the exit interview, I suggested she pursue a job cleaning houses. It didn't require a lot of interaction with people and she could set her own schedule. She told me that cleaning houses was something she had always thought about doing and thanked me for the honest suggestion.

I always want to know how I can help someone, whether they want to grow at Square Donut or it's a temporary position until they can do something they really love. My goal is to listen to what they want, ask questions, and help them personally and professionally. What wisdom can I share that will help them become an even better employee down the road? What wisdom can I share that will help them not just as an employee but as a person? I want to make an impact and leave an impression, no matter how large or small. I want sharing wisdom to be part of my legacy.

Countless times over the years friends or colleagues asked me if their business idea was viable. Most of the time the idea is a passing fancy rather than a sustainable business. For example, if someone says, "I'd love to open a coffee shop on the south side of town," the first question I'd ask is if they have worked at a coffee shop—are they aware of the hours? Next, I'd probably ask why they want one in that particular area of town—do they live there? Do they want to make a little extra money on the side or make a lot of money that can help their kids in the future? A few simple questions quickly reveal whether they want to own a business or if they are truly a business owner. When my son Jack wanted to start a car detailing business, I knew he was serious when he started making a list of necessary items: a business name, logo, business cards, cleaning products, towels, etc. It's easy to talk about the "big picture," but it's difficult to work through the details needed to make the big picture happen. It gets overwhelming when you realize the steps to merely open the doors let alone be successful.

Many people also don't have the risk tolerance, especially financially, to start a business. The ones who do are so busy moving forward with details they don't stop to discuss it with many people. They seek out a specific team of professionals to help them—contractor, attorney, and accountant. Entrepreneurs usually have a small circle helping them get everything in place. When a budding business owner comes to me and I know they are thinking five steps ahead, I try to offer something they haven't yet considered. In the case of a coffee shop owner, I might ask if they've researched where their beans are grown, or who roasts them. I know firsthand that when you're in the throes of starting a business, there are always one or two details you overlook or simply don't know, so I want to help other business owners any way I can.

#ENCOURAGEMENT

In addition to sharing wisdom with employees and with other business owners, I want to be a source of encouragement within my community. There are many ways you can help mentor, educate, and be a resource for organizations and people who need it. I believe that a business shouldn't have feelings or opinions but a business owner can. Because my motivation is bringing people together and providing them a safe, comfortable, happy space, I want my efforts outside of Square Donut to do the same. For example, I serve on an advisory committee for my town's new high school that helps teens experience a particular industry so they can make an informed decision regarding a career they want to pursue. The program provides a way for them to determine if college is the right path. Committee members represent a wide range of industries and perspectives, and it's an amazing way to help teens start to think through details and the steps needed to pursue their dreams.

I'm also passionate about helping local non-profit organizations in my community. One is Project Pink'd, which helps breast cancer survivors thrive after diagnosis. My goal is to collaborate with other small local businesses to support the organization through our products. Another organization important to me is Youth Emergency Services (YES), which helps kids who are homeless or near homeless with emergency shelter, transitioning to independent living, or providing resources for those already living on their own. I know what it's like to grow up without a place that feels like home and without a nurturing adult who can help you find a job or teach you skills. I want to work with YES on a program that teaches kids how to find a job, how to be a good employee, and how to have confidence to pursue a career. I'd love to offer them jobs at Square Donut and help break the cycle of homelessness.

The Special Olympics is also dear to my heart. When I was in the pageant industry, I had the opportunity to work with the Special Olympics, and it was my favorite activity. Not only do I want to supply donuts for the Special Olympics event in my community, I want to play an active role and provide my employees with the opportunity to get involved as well.

No matter if you are around your employees, other business owners, or out in the community, remember that you are always a role model. Your behaviors, actions, decisions, and responses will always be noticed, so let your wisdom be seen through what you do and how you treat others.

Ingredient Tip: Use Wisdom Generously

You've created the recipe for your dreams, now go out and share it with others! Whether that's shared with your employees, people who are starting a business, or through a non-profit organization in your community, you never know who will benefit from your unique experiences. The wisdom you share and the way in which you treat others will be how you're remembered and establish your legacy.

CONCLUSION

Whether you're considering taking the first step toward achieving a dream, are in the middle of your journey, or on the other side of success, you know that every dream requires an incredible amount of work. It's easy to look at other people's lives or businesses and think everything is perfect, especially thanks to social media. I constantly receive comments praising me for my accomplishments or complimenting Square Donut for its cute, clever concept and being an overnight success. When you look behind the lens of the smart phone that took the photo of that "perfect" family, you'll find a husband and wife who argue, kids who get into trouble, or a family who lost a loved one. Similarly, behind every small business that seems to be an overnight success, you'll find a business owner who fought, worked hard, sacrificed, and put their heart and soul into keeping it

Conclusion

going. Whether it's a family or a business, nothing succeeds without having the right ingredients.

Every dream starts with *motivation* and asking yourself, "What do you want, and how badly do you want it?" Whatever it is you desire, you are the only person who can make it happen. Nobody can do it for you, so you have to really want it and do the hard work to see it through. No matter your definition of happiness and success, you can't achieve it if you don't have something that continuously motivates you to achieve your dream.

If you want to achieve your dream faster, don't pass up an *opportunity*. Whether you create the opportunity or take advantage of one that comes along, doing so condenses the time it takes to get from point A to point B. Each opportunity provides you with some form of knowledge, skill, or experience that will be applicable toward achieving your goal. Even a job you don't enjoy can teach patience, tolerance, or prioritization skills. One way or another, every opportunity teaches you something.

It's impossible to be successful without *determination*. This means don't ever give up. For me, determination also means I won't lose and will prove the doubters wrong. Determination is fueled by adversity, challenges, and setbacks. You can't let those influences win, and determination is what gets you through them. I refuse to give up because I want to win and cross the bridge to happiness and success, which is where my dream resides.

Conclusion

If you've been told you're not a strong leader, you can change that. *Leadership* can be learned if you're open to it. Leadership has the power to build and the power to destroy. Leaders can either build morale and motivation or they can ruin it, but the ones who know how to build it are the ones who find success. Some people are born leaders and have the ability to recognize people's strengths and weaknesses. They know how to bring a team together to reach a common goal, whether it's immediate, such as a production or customer service goal, or longer term, such as a financial goal. A good leader must genuinely care about their team and trust them enough to step away and let the team members do their job, and in turn, the team trusts that you are doing yours. Creating that boundary enables everyone to do their job better, which results in meeting the shared goal even faster.

Sometimes when nothing else seems to be working, the one ingredient you need is a little *grace*. It's often the only thing that's left when there are no other options. As soon as I embraced grace and gave up debilitating perfectionism, I started to find peace. My reaction to mistakes changed. When a mistake occurred, I was able to embrace it and move on. I had to learn to give myself grace before I could teach it to my employees, but as soon as they saw that making mistakes was okay, they felt less stressed and didn't worry so much about their own mistakes. It gave them strength and confidence, because when you're not pressured to be perfect,

Conclusion

fewer mistakes occur. Grace allows room for listening, learning, and growth for everyone involved.

If there's one ingredient you should never leave home without, it's *self-care*. Often this notion isn't fully understood until later in life, and it's one of the most underrated. You will only reach a fraction of your intended success without self-care. The sooner you recognize that caring for your mind, body, and soul is just as important as caring for others, you will have a bigger impact and be a happier person. Taking care of yourself first is not selfish, it's selfless. You can't take care of your business or the people you care about until you take care of yourself.

One of the greatest survival tools is *optimism*. Not accepting anything less than the best is a great way to approach your dreams. It means you don't want to settle and you know that positive energy is infectious and creates peace, happiness, and ultimately, success. Optimism combats defeat and encourages strong confidence in the future. It requires step-by-step action that leads to measurable results. Remember that it takes less energy to be optimistic than to be negative and cynical—so put that extra energy into achieving your dreams.

Knowledge comes in many forms, but anytime you've learned something you can share with others, you have *wisdom*. My goal for sharing my life experiences, especially as an entrepreneur, is to help identify potential problem areas, so the positive experiences outweigh the negative. I would rather people understand my journey and respect what I've accomplished rather than simply applaud my success. Wisdom is a gift that only has value when shared.

Dreams are crucial to happiness and success. The ingredients discussed in this book are applicable in achieving your own dreams or when helping someone else. Anyone can do it, no matter your upbringing, education, or financial status. Starting from scratch isn't easy, but if you combine the ingredients in this recipe, I'm confident you'll find happiness and success in business to make your dreams comes true.

ACKNOWLEDGMENTS

I would like to thank Carole Sprunk and Kathy Rygg for the encouragement to write this book. They helped me make another of my dreams come to fruition. I'm also grateful to my mother for not giving up when so many times she could have. Square Donut would not have had the opportunity to be born without Dennis McKelvy and his continued guidance and mentorship. Thank you to Jeremy, who introduced me to the donuts that changed my life and led me to Dennis. I am eternally grateful for the customer love Square Donut received through wicked global adversity—thank you for your continued support of small business. And for all the people who witnessed the blood, sweat, and tears (literally) of my journey and believed in me.

ABOUT THE AUTHOR

This is Elizabeth Pooley's first book and one of many she hopes to write. Before writing her story, she went from making butter and milking cows on her grandparent's farm to working in many areas of business, education, and restaurants, all while feeding her entrepreneurial spirit and creating a world in which anyone can achieve success. She currently lives in Bennington, Nebraska, with her dog, Aspen. Follow Square Donut on social media to admire her unique donut creations and to visit her sweet boutique donut shop in Omaha, Nebraska.

Elizabeth's recommended reading:

The 7 Habits of Highly Effective People by Stephen R. Covey

You Are a Badass: How to Stop Doubting Your Greatness and Start Living an Awesome Life by Jen Sincero

Extreme Ownership: How U.S. Navy SEALs Lead and Win by Jocko Willink and Leaf Babin

How to Win Friends and Influence People by Dale Carnegie

www.ingramcontent.com/pod-product-compliance
Lightning Source LLC
Chambersburg PA
CBHW070343010526
44119CB00029B/414/J